The Book of AI & Machine Learning

AI Machine Learning & Python for Students

Abeer Verma

Fusion Books

Publisher	:	**Fusion Books** X-30, Okhla Industrial Area, Phase-II New Delhi-110020
Phone	:	011- 40712200
E-mail	:	wecare@diamondbooks.in
Website	:	www.diamondbooks.in
Edition	:	2026

Author's Note

Artificial Intelligence and Machine Learning are not distant future technologies — they are tools shaping our present.
But understanding AI is not enough.

To truly unlock its power, students must also understand how machine learning models work and how programming languages like Python bring these systems to life.
This book is designed to bridge that gap.

It combines:

- Core AI concepts
- Machine Learning fundamentals
- Neural Networks
- Ethical thinking
- Real-world Indian examples
- And practical Python applications

You don't need to be an expert to begin.
You need curiosity, consistency, and the willingness to build.

My goal is simple:
To help students move from learning about AI to creating with AI.
Let's build the future — responsibly and intelligently.

— Abeer Verma

Preface

AI, ML & Python — The Complete Student Toolkit
Artificial Intelligence is the broad vision.
Machine Learning is the engine.
Python is the tool.
Together, they form the foundation of modern intelligent systems.

This book is written for high school students who want to:

- Understand AI beyond buzzwords
- Learn how machines actually learn
- Explore neural networks and deep learning
- Write Python programs that connect with AI
- Build real-world mini projects
- Think critically about ethics and responsibility

Aligned with NEP 2020 and emerging curriculum standards, this book balances:
Conceptual clarity + Practical implementation.

Rather than overwhelming you with mathematics, this guide focuses on:
Understanding → Application → Reflection → Creation
By the end of this book, you won't just know what AI is.
You will understand how it works — and how to build with it.

Foreword

Artificial Intelligence and Machine Learning are transforming industries at an unprecedented pace.
For today's students, understanding AI is no longer optional — it is foundational.

But true digital literacy requires more than awareness. It requires the ability to:

- Analyze data
- Train models
- Write code
- Question bias
- Build ethical solutions

The Big Book of AI and Machine Learning – AI, Machine Learning & Python for Students integrates theory and practice in a way that empowers learners to become creators.

By connecting core AI concepts with Python programming and real-world examples, this book prepares students not just for examinations — but for the evolving digital economy.
The future belongs to those who understand both intelligence and implementation.
May this book inspire thoughtful innovation.

Table of Contents

Chapter 1

What is Artificial Intelligence?

Understanding Intelligence, Human vs. Machine

The Magic Behind Your Smart Assistant

Imagine this: You wake up and say, "Hey Google, what's the weather today?" Within seconds, your phone responds with the forecast. On your way to school, Google Maps alerts you about a traffic jam and suggests a faster route.

Later, Netflix recommends a show you've never seen before — and you end up loving it.

What's the magic behind all this?

That's Artificial Intelligence — not magic, but a powerful technology that is changing the world around us. In this chapter, we'll explore what AI is, how it works, and why it matters for your future.

Explore the Concept: Understanding AI

What is Artificial Intelligence?

Artificial Intelligence (AI) is the ability of machines to think, learn, and make decisions — just like humans. It's a branch of computer science that focuses on creating systems that can perform tasks that normally require human intelligence.

These tasks include:

• Understanding speech (like Siri or Alexa)
• Recognizing faces (like Face ID)
• Making decisions (like traffic navigation)
• Learning from experience (like YouTube's recommendations)

In short, AI is about making machines smart.

Human Intelligence vs. Artificial Intelligence

Let's compare the two:

Feature	Human Intelligence	Artificial Intelligence
Learning	From experience, emotions, and reasoning	From data and algorithms
Thinking	Based on logic, emotions, ethics	Based on code and data
Adaptability	High (creative, emotional)	Limited (rules/data-driven)
Speed	Slower but intuitive	Fast and consistent

AI doesn't have emotions or common sense like humans — but it can process huge amounts of data faster than any person can.

In the Real World: Where You See AI Today

AI is not just science fiction anymore. It's already everywhere.

Healthcare

• AI helps doctors detect diseases through MRI scans and X-rays.
• During COVID-19, AI was used to track infections and predict outbreaks.

Agriculture

• AI-powered drones monitor crop health and soil conditions.
• Apps like Kisan AI give farmers weather alerts and crop advice.

Education

• AI tutors personalize learning based on your speed and style.
• Platforms like DIKSHA and Bhashini use AI to make education inclusive.

E-commerce

• Amazon recommends products based on your past behavior.
• AI manages chatbots that help with customer service.

Transportation

• Google Maps predicts traffic using real-time data.
• Self-driving cars are being tested globally.

India is also embracing AI. From Aadhaar to UPI to Bhashini, AI is at the heart of our digital revolution.

Try It Yourself: Activities for Learning

Activity 1: Can AI Do This?

Read each task and decide: Can AI do it? (✓or ✗)

Task	AI Can Do This?
Recognize faces	✓
Dream while sleeping	✗
Predict weather	✓
Taste food	✗
Play chess	✓

Activity 2: Teachable Machine Experiment

Go to Teachable Machine by Google.

Try the Image or Audio Project:

1. Train the AI with your facial expressions or voice commands.
2. Test how well it recognizes you.
3. **Think:** How did it learn?

No coding needed — just explore and observe.

Think & Reflect

1. Can AI have emotions like humans? Should it?
2. What could go wrong if AI systems make biased decisions?
3. How would you feel if your teacher was replaced by a robot?

These questions help us think critically about the ethics and impact of AI on society.

Let's Revise: Summary Flowchart

How AI Works – Simple Flow

nginx

CopyEdit

Data → Algorithm → Learning → Output/Decision

Key Points Recap:

• AI = Machine Intelligence

• Learns from data using algorithms

• Already used in daily life (Google Maps, Alexa, etc.)

• Can't feel, but can think (logically)

Check Yourself: Quick Review Quiz

Multiple Choice Questions (MCQs)

1. What does AI stand for?

a) Automatic Interface

b) Advanced Input

c) Artificial Intelligence ✓

d) Actual Intelligence

2. Which of the following is not an example of AI?

a) Siri

b) Netflix Suggestions

c) Flashlight App ✓

d) Face Recognition

Short Answer Questions

• Name two differences between human intelligence and AI.

• Give one use of AI in agriculture.

• What do we mean when we say "AI learns from data"?

Explore a Future in AI: Careers for You

AI isn't just cool — it's a career booster! Some popular roles include:

Career	What They Do
AI Engineer	Designs intelligent systems
Data Scientist	Analyzes data to make decisions
NLP Developer	Works with speech/language AI
AI Ethics Expert	Ensures AI is fair and unbiased

India's AI for Youth initiative is empowering students with skills in AI, ML, and coding — a great head start for future innovators.

Abeer's AI Builder Insight
AI is not magic — it's mathematics, logic, and data working together. If you understand the building blocks clearly at the beginning, every advanced concept later will feel structured instead of overwhelming.

Beyond the Book: Project Idea

Project: "AI in My Community"

Explore how AI is being used in your local area — school, city, village, or online. Interview people, collect pictures, and create a short report or poster.

Questions to answer:

- Where is AI used (e.g., ATMs, online classes)?
- Who benefits from it?
- What problems can AI solve here?

This will help you connect classroom learning to real-world needs.

Chapter 2

The Journey of AI

History, Milestones, and Today's Applications

From Mythology to Machines

Thousands of years ago, humans imagined statues that could speak, think, and act. In Indian epics like the Ramayana and Mahabharata, we hear about flying chariots (Pushpak Viman) and intelligent weapons. Even in Greek mythology, there are stories of mechanical beings built by gods.

What if we told you that those ancient dreams are slowly coming true? This chapter takes you on an exciting journey through time — from ancient imagination to modern-day Artificial Intelligence.

Explore the Concept: History of Artificial Intelligence

What is the history of AI?

AI did not appear overnight. It evolved step by step, powered by advancements in mathematics, logic, engineering, and computer science.

Let's explore key milestones:

Step 1: The Idea of Intelligent Machines (Before 1900s)

• **Myths & Stories:** Early tales of artificial beings existed in many cultures.

• **Mechanical Devices:** Ancient Indian and Chinese inventors created simple machines like clocks and automata.

• **Philosophical Thought:** Greek philosophers like Aristotle wrote about logic and reasoning.

Step 2: Birth of Computer Science (1900–1950)

• **George Boole (1850s):** Created Boolean logic — the foundation of computer operations.

• **Alan Turing (1936):** British mathematician who proposed the idea of a "Universal Machine" — later called the Turing Machine — capable of solving any problem.

• **Turing Test (1950):** A test to check if a machine can mimic human behavior so well that a person cannot tell if it's a machine.

Turing's Question: "Can machines think?"

Step 3: Early AI Research (1950s–1970s)

• **1956 – The Birth of AI:** The term "Artificial Intelligence" was officially used for the first time at a conference at Dartmouth College, USA.

• John McCarthy, Marvin Minsky, and others began building early programs to solve puzzles and play games like chess.

• These systems could perform logic tasks but lacked memory and real-world knowledge.

Step 4: The AI Winters (1974–1990s)
AI faced major setbacks due to:

• Lack of computing power
• High cost of development
• Unfulfilled expectations

Governments and investors stopped funding AI research. This period is called the "AI Winter".

But researchers kept working in the background, quietly improving algorithms and.

Step 5: The AI Comeback (1990s–2010)

• Rise of the Internet made huge data available for machines to learn from.
• Improved hardware allowed faster processing.
• **1997:** IBM's Deep Blue defeated world chess champion Garry Kasparov — a historic moment!
• AI started to appear in homes — virtual pets, mobile games, and early chatbots.

Step 6: AI Everywhere (2010–Present)

• **2011:** Apple launched Siri, the voice assistant.
• **2016:** Google's AlphaGo defeated a world champion at Go — a game more complex than chess.
• **Today:** AI is in healthcare, banking, transportation, agriculture, and more.
• In India, initiatives like AI for Bharat, Bhashini, and India Stack are leading global examples.

In the Real World: India's AI Timeline

Let's look at how India has embraced AI:

Year	Milestone
2009	Aadhaar project launched – one of the largest biometric databases
2016	UPI payment system launched using data intelligence
2018	NITI Aayog released National AI Strategy: #AIforAll
2022	Launch of Bhashini – AI-powered language platform
2023	AI introduced as a CBSE subject in schools

Try It Yourself: Time Travel with AI

Activity 1: Create a Timeline

Draw a timeline from 1950 to 2025 and mark the following events:

- Turing Machine
- Dartmouth Conference
- Deep Blue vs. Kasparov
- Launch of Siri
- India's AI for All initiative

Use colors or visuals to make your timeline attractive.

Activity 2: Play a Game with an AI Bot

Visit a chess website like lichess.org or playrobot.org and play a game against an AI bot. After the game, ask yourself:

• How did the AI respond?
• Did it learn from your moves?
• Was it smarter than you expected?

Think & Reflect

1. Why did AI face a "winter" despite early success?
2. Can you think of an Indian invention that uses AI?
3. What if AI had been developed 100 years earlier — how might history have changed?

Let's Revise: Mind Map

scss

CopyEdit

```
HISTORY OF AI

│
├── Ancient Imagination (Myths & Legends)
├── Turing & Logic (1930s–50s)
├── Early AI Programs (1956–70s)
├── AI Winter (1974–90s)
├── AI Comeback (1990s–2010)
└── AI Explosion (2011–Present)
```

Key Points:

• AI has evolved over nearly a century
• Important contributions from math, logic, and computer science
• India is now a leader in AI applications for the public

Check Yourself: Quick Review Quiz

MCQs

1. Who is considered the "father of AI"?

a) Isaac Newton

b) John McCarthy ✓

c) Albert Einstein

d) Alan Turing

2. What is the Turing Test used for?

a) Testing human IQ

b) Measuring internet speed

c) Checking if a machine can think like a human ✓

d) Comparing programming languages

3. Which of the following happened in 1997?

a) Siri was launched

b) AI Winter began

c) Deep Blue defeated Garry Kasparov ✓

d) Bhashini launched

Short Questions

- What is meant by "AI Winter"?
- Name two contributions of India in the field of AI.
- What was the Dartmouth Conference?

Explore a Future in AI: Become an AI Historian

Careers Related to This Chapter:

- AI Researcher – Studies new ways for machines to learn
- Digital Historian – Tracks technology evolution and impact

• AI Policy Advisor – Helps governments regulate AI growth
• Science Communicator – Writes and teaches about AI's history
These careers combine curiosity, writing, research, and technology.

Beyond the Book: Project Idea

Project: "AI in Indian Mythology and History"
Research how ancient Indian texts or tools imagined intelligent beings or machines. Examples:

- Pushpak Viman (a flying machine)
- Mechanical toys in ancient temples
- Iron Pillar of Delhi (advanced metallurgy)

Make a presentation linking those ideas to modern AI.

Chapter 3

AI Around Us

Domains of AI (Data, Computer Vision, NLP) and Indian Use Cases

Is AI Only in Robots?

When you hear “AI,” what comes to mind? A robot? A talking machine? Maybe a sci-fi movie character?

What if we told you that AI is already around you — every day, every hour, and sometimes even without you noticing?

• That YouTube video recommendation? AI.
• Google Maps’ traffic update? AI.
• Your face unlock on your phone? Also AI.

In this chapter, we explore how AI is quietly working in the background — in your home, school, city, and even your favorite games.

Explore the Concept: Understanding Domains of AI

AI is not just one technology — it is a combination of many domains. Each domain helps machines "understand" a different type of information: images, words, numbers, or actions.
Let's look at the three key domains of Artificial Intelligence:

1. Data (Structured and Unstructured)

Data is the fuel of AI.
Every time you watch a video, click a link, or like a photo — you generate data. AI systems use this data to learn your preferences, predict your needs, or take actions.

Examples:

- Netflix uses watch history to recommend movies.
- E-commerce sites use purchase data to suggest products.
- Schools use test scores and attendance data to track performance.

Real-world Analogy: Just like a chef needs ingredients to cook, AI needs data to work.

2. Computer Vision (CV)

This domain helps machines see and understand images or videos, just like our eyes and brain do together.

Examples:

- Face ID on phones
- Security cameras that detect motion
- Self-driving cars that recognize traffic signs
- Medical AI that reads X-rays and scans

Fun Fact: Computer Vision helped farmers in Maharashtra detect crop diseases using drone images and AI apps.

3. Natural Language Processing (NLP)

NLP enables computers to understand and respond to human language — both spoken and written.

Examples:

- Virtual assistants like Siri, Google Assistant, and Alexa
- Google Translate
- Chatbots on websites
- Speech-to-text typing

NLP also includes:

- NLU (Natural Language Understanding) – how machines understand meaning
- NLG (Natural Language Generation) – how machines reply in human-like language

Indian Example: Bhashini is India's AI-powered platform that breaks language barriers and translates content in multiple Indian languages using NLP.

In the Real World: AI in Everyday Life

Let's explore how AI is transforming different sectors:

Healthcare

- AI diagnoses diseases from medical scans (like X-rays, MRIs).
- Chatbots help answer patient queries.
- Predictive models can warn doctors about future health risks.

Agriculture

• Drones and sensors use AI to detect crop health.
• Soil data helps farmers decide when to irrigate.
• Market price prediction tools support better decision-making.

Education

• Personalized learning apps adjust content based on student speed and accuracy.
• AI auto-checks multiple-choice exams.
• Virtual tutors provide 24x7 doubt-solving.

Retail & E-commerce

• Online stores recommend items based on your browsing behavior.
• AI manages stock and inventory in warehouses.
• Virtual try-on tools in fashion and makeup apps.

Government and Public Services

• Facial recognition used in security systems.
• AI chatbots on government portals.
• Smart traffic lights adjust signals based on real-time flow.

Social Media

• Content moderation using AI to block hate speech or fake news.
• Filters and stickers use facial detection (Computer Vision).
• AI suggests hashtags or edits photos automatically.

Try It Yourself: Let AI Do the Thinking

Activity 1: Match the Domain

Match each AI example with the correct domain:

AI Task	Domain
Recommending songs	Data
Face unlock	Computer Vision
Translating Hindi to English	NLP
Diagnosing X-rays	Computer Vision
Detecting fake news	NLP + Data

Try making your own examples and share them in class!

Activity 2: Use Google Lens or Teachable Machine

- Open the Google Lens app.
- Point it at any object — a book, flower, or animal.
- What did AI detect?

Or go to Teachable Machine, upload 3 images, and train your own image recognition model — no coding required!

Think & Reflect

1. Can AI ever understand emotions like humans?
2. Is it fair to let AI decide who gets a job interview?
3. What should be the limit for AI in our personal lives?

These questions help us reflect on ethics, privacy, and trust in AI systems.

Let’s Revise: Flowchart Summary

markdown

CopyEdit

```
      DOMAINS OF AI
              |
   ┌──────────┼──────────┐
   |          |          |
Data      Computer     NLP
           Vision
```

Key Recap:

- **Data:** AI learns from user behavior, choices, and feedback.
- **Computer Vision:** AI sees and interprets images and video.
- **NLP:** AI understands and generates human language.

Check Yourself: Quick Quiz

MCQs

1. Which AI domain powers Google Translate?

a) Computer Vision

b) Data

c) NLP ✓

d) Robotics

2. What does Computer Vision help machines do?

a) Hear sounds

b) Understand images ✓

c) Create art

d) Learn coding

3. Which platform is India's initiative for language AI?

a) ChatGPT

b) Alexa

c) Bhashini ✓

d) Aarogya Setu

Short Answer Questions

- What are the three major domains of AI?
- How does AI help in agriculture?
- Give two examples of NLP from your daily life.

Explore a Future in AI: Careers from Every Domain

Each domain of AI opens the door to different careers:

Domain	Career Options
Data	Data Scientist, AI Analyst
Computer Vision	Computer Vision Engineer, Robotics Expert
NLP	Speech Recognition Developer, Chat-bot Designer

Did You Know? India is expected to create over 10 lakh jobs in AI and related fields by 2030.

Beyond the Book: Project Idea

Project: "AI in My Day"

Document how many times you interact with AI in a day.

Make a list:

- **Wake up:** Voice assistant
- **School:** Google search, chatbots
- **Evening:** Netflix suggestions, Face unlock

Create a poster or digital timeline titled "A Day in the Life with AI" and present it to your class.

Chapter 4

Ethics and Responsibility

Bias, Privacy, Safety, and Fairness in AI

Can a Machine Be Biased?

Imagine you're applying for a college scholarship. The application is judged by an AI system. You meet all the requirements,
But the system rejects you. Later, you find out that it was trained mostly on data from other regions and ignored your state's achievements.

Was it fair?

AI is powerful — but not perfect. That's why we need to talk about ethics, bias, and responsible use.

Explore the Concept: What is Ethics in AI?

Ethics means understanding the difference between right and wrong

— and making fair, safe, and respectful decisions. When we apply ethics to machines,

we ask:

• Are AI systems fair to everyone?
• Are they safe and secure?
• Do they respect privacy?
• Can they explain how they make decisions?

This is called Ethical AI or Responsible AI.

Why Does AI Need Ethics?

Unlike humans, AI does not have emotions, culture, or conscience. It follows instructions and learns from data. But what if the data is incomplete, biased, or harmful?

Problems That Can Happen Without Ethics:

1. Bias in AI

o If an AI is trained only on data from a certain gender, language, or region, it may be unfair to others.
o Example: A job recruitment AI that prefers male applicants because its training data had mostly male resumes.

2. Lack of Privacy

o AI systems often collect personal data like location, age, or voice.
o If not protected, this data can be misused.

3. Lack of Transparency

o Sometimes, even the creators of AI systems can't fully explain how the AI made a decision. This is called a "black box" problem.

4. Dependence and Job Loss

o Overuse of AI may reduce the need for human workers, especially in repetitive jobs.

5. Misinformation

o AI tools can generate fake videos (deepfakes), fake news, and spam.

Principles of Responsible AI

1. Fairness

• Treat all users equally regardless of race, gender, age, or location.

• Example: Translation tools should work for all Indian languages, not just Hindi or English.

2. Privacy

• Protect user data and avoid surveillance without consent.

• Example: A health app using AI should not share personal medical data with advertisers.

3. Explainability

• The system should explain its decision-making process in simple language.

4. Accountability

• If AI makes a mistake, someone should be responsible — developer, company, or user.

5. Sustainability

• Use AI in a way that supports the environment and society.

In the Real World: Ethical Dilemmas in AI

Let's look at examples from India and the world:

Facial Recognition at Airports

Some Indian airports use facial recognition to speed up check-in. But what if:

• It fails to recognize faces with dark skin tones?
• It stores your photo without permission?
Ethical Question: Is it okay to trade privacy for speed?

WhatsApp Forward Detection

AI helps flag fake news on WhatsApp. But what if:

• It wrongly labels a true news report as fake?
• It censors voices from minority groups?
Ethical Question: Who decides what's real?

AI Chatbots in Schools

Some schools are using AI chatbots for homework help. But what if:

• Students misuse them for cheating?
• The bot gives wrong or biased answers?
Ethical Question: Can AI replace teachers?

Try It Yourself: Ethics in Action

Activity 1: AI Dilemma Debate
Your AI system has to choose between:

- Saving one passenger inside a self-driving car
- Or swerving and hitting a group of 3 pedestrians

Who should it save?

Divide into two teams:

- Team A defends the car's choice to save its passenger.
- Team B defends saving the pedestrians.

Debate and then reflect on the challenges of ethical programming.

Activity 2: AI Bias Test (with Teachable Machine)
Use Teachable Machine:

- Train it to recognize two kinds of objects (e.g., pens and books).
- Give it more photos of one object than the other.

Observe how the model becomes biased. Discuss why balanced data is important.

Think & Reflect

1. Should AI systems always tell us how they make decisions?
2. What should be done if an AI makes a life-changing mistake?
3. Can AI ever be completely fair and neutral?

Let's Revise: Mind Map Summary

markdown
CopyEdit
RESPONSIBLE AI

FAIRNESS
PRIVACY
EXPLAINABLE
ACCOUNTABLE

Quick Recap:

- Ethics means making fair, respectful, and safe choices.
- AI can have bias if trained on limited data.
- Responsible AI is fair, private, explainable, accountable, and sustainable.
- Ethics help us build AI that works for everyone.

Check Yourself: Quick Quiz

MCQs

1. What is a common ethical concern in AI?
a) AI moving too slowly
b) AI solving math problems
c) AI being biased toward certain groups ✓
d) AI learning new languages

2. What does "black box" in AI mean?
a) A storage box
b) An unknown algorithm ✓
c) A coding error
d) A robot's body

3. What is "explainable AI"?

a) AI that gives answers in English
b) AI that explains its decisions ✓
c) AI that speaks politely
d) AI that explains laws

Short Answer Questions

- Name any two ethical concerns related to AI.
- What does "AI bias" mean? Give an example.
- Why is privacy important in AI systems?

Explore a Future in AI: Ethics and Beyond

As AI becomes more common, careers in AI ethics are growing fast.

Role	What They Do
AI Ethicist	Ensures AI follows moral principles
Policy Maker	Builds laws around AI use
AI Researcher	Creates fair and safe AI tools
Data Auditor	Checks if data is balanced and private

AI + Law + Logic = Great Career for Future Leaders!

Beyond the Book: Project Idea

Project: Build an AI Code of Ethics for Your School

Imagine your school is getting a new AI system for:

- Facial attendance
- Smart grading

• Chatbot-based doubt solving

Create a "Student Code of AI Ethics" that includes:

• Privacy rules
• Fair use policy
• Student rights and responsibilities

Design a poster or brochure and share with your classmates or school IT team.

Chapter 5

Machine Learning Basics

How Machines Learn with Data

Can a Machine Learn Like You?

Imagine you're learning how to recognize different types of birds. At first,

Someone shows you pictures and names them: pigeon, crow, sparrow. After seeing many examples, you start identifying birds on your own — even new ones you haven't seen before.

Now imagine training a computer to do the same. That's machine learning — teaching machines to learn from data just like you learn from experience.

In this chapter, you'll discover how Machine Learning (ML) helps AI systems become "smart" by using data to improve over time.

Explore the Concept: What is Machine Learning?

Machine Learning (ML)

Machine Learning is a subset of Artificial Intelligence where machines are trained to learn from data instead of being explicitly programmed.

Instead of writing step-by-step rules for everything, we:

- Feed the machine lots of examples (data)
- Let it learn patterns
- And use those patterns to make predictions or decisions

Definition: "Machine Learning is the science of getting computers to learn without being explicitly programmed." – Arthur Samuel (1959)

Example to Understand ML

Let's say we want to train a machine to recognize fruits.

Image	Feature 1: Color	Feature 2: Size	Label
Apple	Red	Medium	Apple
Banana	Yellow	Long	Banana
Orange	Orange	Round	Orange

The machine learns patterns:

- If color = yellow and size = long → it's likely a banana.

This is how ML works — it uses features and data to learn and predict outcomes.

Types of Machine Learning

1. Supervised Learning

In supervised learning:

- We train the machine using labeled data (data with answers).
- The model learns from input-output pairs.

Example:

- **Input:** A photo of a cat
- **Output:** "Cat"
- **Input:** A photo of a dog
- **Output:** "Dog"

After training on hundreds of labeled images, the model can label new images accurately.

Use cases:

- Spam email detection
- Face recognition
- Predicting exam scores

2. Unsupervised Learning

In unsupervised learning:

- The data is not labeled
- The machine tries to find hidden patterns or groups (clusters) on its own.

Example:

- A shopping website groups users based on buying habits.
- The machine might group buyers into: gadget lovers, book readers, or fashion fans.

Use cases:

- Customer segmentation
- Market research
- Organizing photos or files

3. Reinforcement Learning

In this type:

- The machine learns by trial and error
- It receives rewards or punishments based on actions

Example:

- A robot tries to walk. If it falls → punishment. If it moves forward → reward.
- Over time, it learns the best way to walk.

Use cases:

- Self-driving cars
- Game-playing bots (like AlphaGo)
- Industrial robots

In the Real World: ML in Action

Healthcare

- Predicting patient risk based on symptoms
- Analyzing scans (X-rays, MRIs) for diseases

Banking

- Detecting fraud by analyzing transaction patterns
- Approving or rejecting loan applications

Smartphones

• Personalized keyboard suggestions
• Voice assistants learning your preferences

E-commerce

• Recommending products based on previous purchases
• Classifying reviews as positive or negative

Indian Example:

The Aarogya Setu app used machine learning to identify COVID-19 hotspots based on user data and symptoms.

Try It Yourself: Let's Build a Mini ML Model

Activity 1: Sorting Shapes

1. Collect paper cutouts of different shapes (circles, squares, triangles).
2. Label each one.
3. Let your friend (the "machine") observe patterns.
4. Now give them a new shape and ask them to guess — have they learned?

This mimics supervised learning.

Activity 2: Teachable Machine by Google

Go to: https://teachablemachine.withgoogle.com

1. Click on Image Project.
2. Add images of two objects (like books vs bottles).
3. Train the model.
4. Test it with new images.

You've just created an image classification model using supervised learning!

Think & Reflect

1. Can machines ever learn like humans — with emotions and context?
2. If an ML model makes a wrong prediction, who is responsible?
3. Is it ethical to use your personal data to train a model without asking?

Let's Revise: Visual Summary

mathematica
CopyEdit
```
MACHINE LEARNING
├── Supervised Learning → Labeled data
├── Unsupervised Learning → Pattern discovery
└── Reinforcement Learning → Rewards & actions
```

Key Concepts Recap:

- Machine Learning = AI that learns from data
- Uses patterns, examples, and feedback
- Major types: Supervised, Unsupervised, Reinforcement
- Powers apps, websites, medical tools, and more

Check Yourself: Quick Quiz

MCQs

1. What type of learning uses labeled data?

a) Reinforcement
b) Supervised ✓
c) Unsupervised
d) Untrained

2. Which is an example of Unsupervised Learning?
a) Identifying handwriting
b) Clustering customers based on shopping ✓
c) Translating text
d) Diagnosing diseases

3. What is the first step in Machine Learning?
a) Writing code
b) Collecting data ✓
c) Buying a robot
d) Printing results

Short Answer Questions
• Define Machine Learning in your own words.
• Name two real-life uses of ML.
• What is the difference between supervised and unsupervised learning?

Explore a Future in AI: Careers in Machine Learning

If you like patterns, logic, and problem-solving, ML offers exciting career paths:

Role	What They Do
ML Engineer	Builds models to make predictions
Data Analyst	Analyzes large datasets
AI Trainer	Prepares training data and refines models
Robotics Programmer	Uses ML to power smart robots

Tip: You can start learning ML with free platforms like Google's AI Hub or India's ATL Tinkering Labs.

> **Abeer's AI Builder Insight**
> Machine Learning doesn't "understand" data the way humans do. It finds patterns. Your job as a builder is to ensure the patterns it learns are meaningful, clean, and fair.

Beyond the Book: Project Idea

Project: "ML at Work in My Life"

Create a log of how Machine Learning interacts with you in one day.

- What music did your app recommend?
- Did YouTube suggest videos?
- Did your phone auto-correct your typing?

Document 5 examples and explain what kind of ML might be involved.

Chapter 6

Smart Coding with Python

Your First Step into AI Programming

Why Python Is the Language of AI

Meet Anaya, a student just like you. She's fascinated by AI and dreams of creating a chatbot to help students revise for exams. But she doesn't know where to start. A teacher introduces her to Python, and suddenly, the world of coding opens up — easy, fun, and full of possibilities. Python isn't just a programming language. It's the language of Artificial Intelligence. In this chapter, you'll learn why Python is so important, how to write your first lines of code, and how it connects to machine learning and AI projects.

Explore the Concept: What is Python?

Python: Simple, Powerful, and Popular

Python is a high-level, beginner-friendly programming language that is widely used in data science, AI, web development, and more.

Why Python for AI?

Feature	Why It Helps in AI
Easy to learn	Simple syntax like English
Huge community	Thousands of tutorials and libraries
AI Libraries	Tools like TensorFlow, Keras, Scikit-learn
Versatile	Used in web apps, automation, and robotics

Python lets you focus on logic, not just writing complicated code.

Basic Concepts in Python

Let's explore the building blocks of Python programming.

1. Printing Messages

python

CopyEdit

```
print("Hello, AI World!")
```

This command tells Python to display a message. It's your first step to communicating with the machine.

2. Variables and Data Types

Variables store information.

python

CopyEdit

```
name = "Anaya"      # Text (String)
age = 15            # Whole number (Integer)
```

temperature = 37.5   # Decimal (Float)
Python automatically understands the type of data.

3. Taking User Input

python
CopyEdit
name = input("What is your name? ")
print("Welcome,", name)
You can now interact with the user — a big part of AI interfaces.

4. If-Else Conditions

These help machines make decisions.
python
CopyEdit
age = int(input("Enter your age: "))
if age >= 18:
    print("You are eligible to vote.")

else:
    print("You are not eligible yet.")
This is how logic and decision-making work — the core of AI.

5. Loops: Repeating Tasks

python
CopyEdit

for i in range(5):
    print("This is loop number", i)
Loops allow the program to repeat actions, just like machines repeat training tasks in ML.

6. Lists: Storing Data in Groups

python
CopyEdit
```
fruits = ["apple", "banana", "mango"]
print(fruits[1])  # Output: banana
```
Lists are like mini-databases, useful in storing datasets for training AI.

In the Real World: Python in AI Projects

Python powers major AI tools and platforms:

Healthcare

• Models that predict diseases use Python for data cleaning, training, and predictions.

Banking

• Python is used to detect fraud by analyzing user behavior.

Education

• EdTech tools (like AI chatbots and adaptive quizzes) are coded in Python.

Indian Example:

The Bhashini language platform uses Python-based models to convert Indian languages in real-time for accessibility.

Try It Yourself: Let's Write Code

Activity 1: Your First Python Chat

python
CopyEdit

name = input("What's your name? ")
feeling = input("How are you feeling today? ")
print("Hi", name + ", I'm glad you're feeling", feeling)

This is the beginning of a chatbot-like program!

Activity 2: AI Guessing Game

python

CopyEdit

```
import random
number = random.randint(1, 10)
guess = int(input("Guess a number between 1 and 10: "))
if guess == number:
    print("Correct!")
```

else:

```
    print("Wrong. The number was", number)
```

This mini-AI program generates random numbers and gives feedback — just like game bots do.

Think & Reflect

1. Can a program written in Python understand your emotions?
2. How can programming influence the fairness of an AI tool?
3. If you built an AI tutor, what would you want it to do?

Let's Revise: Python in a Nutshell

scss

CopyEdit

```
PYTHON BASICS
├── print() → Display messages
├── input() → Take user input
```

```
├── if-else → Make decisions
├── loops → Repeat tasks
├── lists → Store multiple items
└── variables → Store information
```

Recap Points:

• Python is simple and powerful — perfect for beginners and pros.
• Core skills include printing, input, logic, and loops.
• Used in all major AI tools and platforms.
• India's EdTech and health sectors rely heavily on Python.

Check Yourself: Quick Quiz

MCQs

1.What does the print() function do in Python?

a) Runs the program
b) Displays text ✓
c) Takes input
d) Stores numbers

2. Which one is a valid Python variable name?

a) 2name
b) name2 ✓
c) name!
d) first name

3. Why is Python widely used in AI?

a) It's old
b) It has a long syntax

c) It is simple and has AI libraries ✓
d) It doesn't support visuals

Short Answer Questions

- What is a variable? Give an example.
- Write a small Python code to greet the user.
- How is Python connected to Artificial Intelligence?

Explore a Future in AI: Careers in Python Programming

Python opens the door to various AI and tech careers:

Career	Role
Python Developer	Builds applications and tools
Data Scientist	Analyzes data using Python
ML Engineer	Develops models in Python
AI Researcher	Creates AI frameworks and tools

Tip: Explore platforms like Google Colab, Jupyter Notebook, and CodeChef to start coding online!

Abeer's AI Builder Insight

Python is powerful not because it is complicated — but because it is readable. Focus on writing clean, understandable code. Future-you will thank present-you.

Beyond the Book: Project Idea

Project:
Build a Python Quiz Bot

Create a program that:
- Asks 5 questions
- Takes user input
- Gives a score at the end

Example:

```
python
CopyEdit
score = 0
q1 = input("What is the capital of India? ")
if q1.lower() == "delhi":
    score += 1
print("Your score is", score)
```

Upgrade it to add multiple questions, use lists, and give feedback!

Chapter 7

Neural Networks and Beyond

How Machines 'Think' Like Humans

Can a Machine Think Like a Brain?

Have you ever wondered how humans recognize a face instantly? Or how we learn from experience — like not touching a hot pan twice? Now imagine a machine trying to do the same. That's where Neural Networks come in — they help machines "think" by mimicking how our brain works. In this chapter, we'll explore what neural networks are, how they learn from data, and how they're powering AI tools you use every day.

Explore the Concept: What Are Neural Networks?

Inspired by the Human Brain

Our brain has billions of neurons — tiny cells that pass signals to each other. That's how we recognize voices, feel emotions, or remember a song.

A Neural Network in AI tries to replicate this structure using:

• Nodes (artificial neurons) – Like brain cells
• Layers – Input, Hidden, and Output
• Connections (weights) – Strength of signals between nodes

Each node processes information and passes it on — just like a human neuron!

How a Neural Network Works

Let's break it into steps:

1. Input Layer
  o Receives raw data (e.g., pixels of an image or words in a sentence)

2. Hidden Layers
  o Perform calculations, pattern recognition, and decision-making
  o More layers = more complex thinking

3. Output Layer
  o Gives the final result (e.g., "Cat" or "Dog")

Example:

Imagine you're building a model to recognize handwritten digits (0–9).

• **Input:** Image of the digit "3"
• **Hidden layers:** Analyze curves, lines, patterns
• **Output:** Predicts it is a "3" with 95% confidence

Real-Life Analogy

Think of a Neural Network like a school system:

• Input layer = Students entering the school

• Hidden layers = Teachers and classes where learning happens

• Output layer = Final exam result

More students + better teachers = more accurate results!

Types of Neural Networks

1. Feedforward Neural Network

o Basic type where information flows in one direction

o Used in speech and image recognition

2. Convolutional Neural Network (CNN)

o Best for image data

o Used in facial recognition, X-ray analysis, etc.

3. Recurrent Neural Network (RNN)

o Best for sequential data like text or time series

o Used in language translation, chatbots, stock predictions

In the Real World: Neural Networks at Work

Neural networks power many tools you use every day:

Smartphones

• Face unlock uses CNNs

• Voice assistants use RNNs to understand sentences

Healthcare

• AI scans X-rays and MRIs for diseases like cancer

• Predicts patient risk using past health data

Gaming

• Bots learn how to play and improve using trial-and-error neural models

Education

• Personalized AI tutors that adapt to how you learn

Indian Example:

Startups in India are using CNN-based models to detect crop diseases from photos, helping farmers take action early.

Backed by Science: Deep Learning

When a neural network has many hidden layers, it becomes a Deep Neural Network — the core of Deep Learning.

Deep Learning is used in:

• Self-driving cars
• Advanced medical diagnostics
• Real-time language translation
• Chatbots like ChatGPT

Fun Fact: Deep Learning helped AlphaGo defeat a human world champion in the game of Go — a milestone in AI history.

Try It Yourself: Train a Tiny Neural Network

Activity 1: Teachable Machine – Sound or Image Classifier

Go to https://teachablemachine.withgoogle.com

Steps:

1. Create an image or sound project.
2. Train it using 2–3 categories (e.g., clapping vs. silence).
3. Test it live — see how accurate your model is!

This uses a mini neural network in your browser!

Activity 2: Neural Network Paper Model

Draw three layers of circles on paper:

• 3 input nodes

• 4 hidden nodes

• 1 output node

Use string or lines to connect them. Label weights and show how signals pass through. This helps you visualize how machines "think."

Think & Reflect

1. Can a neural network become more intelligent than a human?
2. How do you feel about machines learning from your data?
3. What problems should never be left to AI alone?

Let's Revise: Summary Diagram

scss

CopyEdit

```
NEURAL NETWORK STRUCTURE
Input Layer → Hidden Layers → Output Layer
        (learn)       (predict)
```

Key Takeaways:

• Neural Networks mimic the human brain.

• They use layers and nodes to process data.

• CNNs handle images, RNNs handle sequences.

• Deep Learning = many layers = powerful models

• Used in facial recognition, chatbots, robots, and more

Check Yourself: Quick Quiz

MCQs

1. What part of the human body inspired neural networks?

a) Heart

b) Neurons in the brain ✓

c) Lungs

d) Eyes

2. Which type of neural network is best for image recognition?

a) RNN

b) CNN ✓

c) FNN

d) SVM

3. What is a Deep Neural Network?

a) A basic neural net

b) One with many hidden layers ✓

c) A robot's memory

d) A slow program

Short Answer Questions

- What are the three layers of a neural network?
- How is Deep Learning different from simple ML?
- Give one real-world example of CNN use in India.

Explore a Future in AI: Neural Network Careers

As neural networks evolve, so do careers in this space:

Career	Role
Deep Learning Engineer	Builds multi-layer AI models
AI Researcher	Explores new algorithms

Data Scientist	Applies neural models to real-world problems
ML Model Trainer	Prepares training datasets for neural nets

Tip: Platforms like TensorFlow, Keras, and PyTorch are popular tools for neural networks — and they're all in Python!

Abeer's AI Builder Insight
A neural network is just layers of simple mathematical decisions stacked together. Don't fear the word "neural." Break it into layers, inputs, weights, and outputs — and it becomes logical.

Beyond the Book: Project Idea

Project: "Design Your Own AI Assistant"
Use basic Python and Teachable Machine to:

• Train your assistant to respond to sound (like a clap or your name)
• Add logic in Python to perform tasks (like print a message or open a website)

Optional:

• Use Scratch + ML Extensions for younger learners
This blends logic + data + learning — just like neural networks.

Chapter 8

AI for the Future

Careers, Sustainable Development, and Capstone Ideas

Will AI Take Over the Future?

Sana is 17 and wants to become an architect. Her cousin Rishi wants to be a doctor. But both wonder — will AI take away their jobs? Or can AI become their assistant instead?

What if AI could help architects design smarter buildings, or doctors detect diseases faster?
The truth is — AI will not replace humans, but humans who understand AI will replace those who don't.

In this chapter, we'll explore the future of AI, how it connects with sustainability and responsible citizenship, and the skills and careers young people need to thrive in the AI-powered world ahead.

Explore the Concept:
What Does the AI Future Look Like?

AI is not just a tool — it's a transformative force that will reshape:

- Jobs
- Industries
- Governments
- Education
- The environment

Let's understand how.

Future Careers in AI

You don't need to be a coder to work in AI. The field needs artists, teachers, doctors, writers, lawyers, linguists, and more — all working with AI.

Career Fields and Roles

Domain	Role
Healthcare	AI-assisted doctor, medical data analyst
Agriculture	Precision farming analyst, drone technician
Education	EdTech designer, AI tutor developer
Media & Writing	Content moderator, AI story generator
Government	AI policy maker, digital governance expert
Environment	AI for climate forecasting, conservation robotics

Indian Example: Kisan AI helps farmers decide what to grow, and Bhashini helps people connect across languages.

AI and Sustainable Development

Sustainability means using resources wisely so future generations can thrive.

AI can help in many ways:

1. Agriculture

• AI predicts crop diseases and rainfall

• Helps reduce fertilizer and water waste

2. Energy

• AI systems optimize electricity grids

• Smart homes adjust lighting and temperature

3. Transport

• AI reduces traffic, saves fuel, lowers emissions

4. Climate Change

• Satellite AI tracks forest cover and pollution levels

• Forecasts disasters and supports relief planning

India's AI for All mission links AI with the United Nations Sustainable Development Goals (SDGs).

21st Century Skills You Need for an AI Future

To succeed in the future, you need more than just tech skills. You need:

Skill	Why It Matters
Critical Thinking	Question AI decisions and biases

Problem-Solving	Use AI to solve real-world challenges
Creativity	Build new apps, bots, and solutions
Communication	Explain AI ideas to others
Collaboration	Work with diverse teams and roles
Ethics	Ensure AI is fair and safe

These are called 21st-century competencies, and they're central to NEP 2020 and NCF 2023.

Responsible AI Citizenship

In a world filled with AI tools, you must be more than a user — you must be a responsible digital citizen.

Your Roles:

- Understand how your data is used
- Be alert about misinformation or deepfakes
- Use AI for good — not harm
- Report misuse or unfair AI behavior

Your Rights:

- Right to digital privacy
- Right to transparent AI
- Right to fair use of technology

Responsible citizenship + ethical AI = safer, smarter world

Try It Yourself: Shape the Future

Activity 1: Design an AI Career Poster

Pick a field you're interested in (e.g., music, sports, medicine).

Create a poster that answers:

- How is AI used in this field?
- What careers will emerge?
- What skills will you need?

Display your poster in class and discuss it with peers.

Activity 2: AI for Earth Challenge

Pick a local problem: water shortage, pollution, traffic, etc.

Now brainstorm:

- How can AI help solve this?
- What data would it need?
- Who would use the solution?

Write a 1-page idea pitch — you might just launch your first green startup!

Think & Reflect

1. Will AI reduce jobs or create new ones?
2. Should AI systems follow rules written by people from one culture or country?
3. What is your role in making sure AI is used responsibly?

Let's Revise: AI Future at a Glance

sql

CopyEdit

```
THE FUTURE WITH AI
├── New Careers
│   ├── AI in every field
```

```
│   └── Cross-disciplinary roles
├── Sustainability
│   ├── AI for crops, climate, clean energy
├── Skills Needed
│   ├── Thinking, coding, creating, leading
└── Responsible Citizenship
    ├── Ethics, privacy, fairness
```

Check Yourself: Quick Quiz

MCQs

1. Which of these is NOT a 21st-century skill?

a) Memorization ✓

b) Creativity

c) Problem-solving

d) Collaboration

2. AI can help reduce pollution by:

a) Creating more smoke

b) Optimizing traffic ✓

c) Replacing windmills

d) Blocking roads

3. What does a responsible AI citizen do?

a) Spams chatbots

b) Hacks facial data

c) Reports AI misuse ✓

d) Copies homework from AI

Short Answer Questions

- Name two jobs AI might create in your field of interest.
- How does AI help in climate change?
- Why is it important to learn ethics in AI?

Explore a Future in AI: You Can Lead the Change

Whether you want to be a coder, designer, farmer, filmmaker, or teacher — AI is for you.

The world needs:

- AI changemakers
- Ethical thinkers
- Tech-positive leaders
- Problem solvers with heart

Learn AI. Use it for good. Change the world — one smart solution at a time.

Beyond the Book: Project Idea

Project: "AI for India 2047"

India will complete 100 years of independence in 2047. Imagine a better India powered by AI.

- What problems have been solved?
- What new technologies exist?
- What role did you play?

Create a vision document or creative poster: "My India 2047 – Powered by AI"

Present it in school on Independence Day or Science Exhibition Day.

Chapter 9

AI in India

From Innovation to Inclusion

India's AI Journey

In a small village in Rajasthan, a farmer uses a mobile app that tells him when to water his crops. In Bengaluru, a startup builds an AI tool that translates Tamil into English instantly. In Delhi, students use an AI-powered app to prepare for exams. India is not just using AI — it's building it, adapting it, and sharing it.

This chapter explores how India is becoming a global leader in AI for inclusion, innovation, and impact.

Explore the Concept: India's AI Vision National Strategy for AI

In 2018, NITI Aayog released India's official AI strategy titled:

“#AIforAll” – to ensure AI benefits every citizen, not just a few.

Key Goals:

• Boost agriculture productivity
• Improve healthcare access
• Strengthen education
• Drive smart mobility
• Enhance digital governance

India’s focus is on AI that solves real-world problems for its diverse population.

Key Projects and Initiatives

1. Bhashini

• AI-based language platform that translates between Indian languages in real time
• Makes government services and digital tools inclusive for all

2. India Stack

• Combines Aadhaar, UPI, and DigiLocker to create seamless digital identities
• Used in banking, education, public welfare

3. AI for Youth (CBSE + Intel)

• Introduces AI curriculum in schools from Grade 8 onward
• Encourages students to build solutions for local problems

4. Aarogya Setu

• Used during the COVID-19 pandemic to identify hotspots using AI data modeling

AI Startups & Innovation Hubs

India has a vibrant AI startup ecosystem. Some examples:

Startup	Focus Area
Niramai	AI for early breast cancer detection using thermal imaging
CropIn	AI for farm analytics and crop monitoring
Staqu	Voice-based crime data analysis for police departments
Reverie	Language localization tools using NLP

The government also launched Centers of Excellence in AI in cities like Bengaluru, Hyderabad, and Mumbai to support R&D.

AI in Indian Education

National Education Policy 2020:

- Promotes AI, coding, and computational thinking from an early age
- Encourages project-based, hands-on learning
- Emphasizes ethical use and inclusivity

ATL Labs (Atal Tinkering Labs):

- 10,000+ innovation labs across India where students can build with AI tools and sensors

Try It Yourself: Local AI Challenge

Activity: "AI for My Town"

Pick one issue your community faces — like waste, water, traffic, or education.

Answer:

• How can AI help solve this?

• What data would be needed?

• Can you build a solution using Python or Teachable Machine?

Present your idea as a short video or poster.

Think & Reflect

1. Why does India need AI tools that support multiple languages?
2. Can AI help reduce social inequalities in a diverse country like India?
3. What role can students play in India's AI innovation?

Let's Revise

yaml

CopyEdit

```
INDIA'S AI MISSION
├── #AIforAll (NITI Aayog)
├── Key Platforms: Bhashini, India Stack, UPI
├── Startups: Niramai, CropIn, Staqu
├── Education: AI for Youth, ATL Labs
└── Goals: Health, Education, Farming, Governance
```

Check Yourself

MCQs

1. What is the goal of #AIforAll?

a) AI for only tech companies

b) AI for rural development ✓
c) AI for gaming
d) AI for business only

2. Which app tracked COVID-19 hotspots in India?
a) UPI
b) DigiLocker
c) Aarogya Setu ✓
d) Bhashini

3. What is the purpose of Bhashini?
a) Online payment
b) Language translation ✓
c) Crime detection
d) Climate prediction

Careers from India's AI Movement

Role	Sector
AI Language Specialist	Multilingual tech
AI Policy Advisor	Government & regulation
AI Innovator	Startups & products
AI for Social Good Expert	NGOs, SDG projects

Project Idea:
"Voice for All"

Build or design a prototype that:
- Listens to voice commands in your regional language
- Responds with useful info (weather, school timing, etc.)

Use Teachable Machine + Python + Hindi/Marathi/Bengali input as a starting point.

Chapter 10

Build Your Own AI Project

A Step-by-Step Guide

From Learning to Creating

Imagine telling your teacher: "I built my own AI!"
That moment of pride — watching your idea come alive — is what this chapter is about.
It's time to put your knowledge into action. Whether you're using Teachable Machine, Python, or a mobile app builder, this guide will walk you through building your first real AI project.

Explore the Concept: The AI Project Cycle

Before building, you must think like a creator. AI projects usually follow this 4-step cycle:
markdown

CopyEdit
1. Problem Scoping → 2. Data Acquisition → 3. Model Building → 4. Evaluation
Let's break these down using a real-world example.

Example Project: AI Emotion Detector

What it does:

Uses the webcam to recognize if a person is happy, sad, or neutral — and gives a response like "Cheer up!" or "Keep smiling!"

Step 1: Problem Scoping
Ask yourself:

- What do I want the AI to do?
- Who will use it?
- Why is it useful?

Goal: Help teachers understand students' emotional state in online classes

Users: Teachers and students

Why: To improve engagement and support mental well-being

Step 2: Data Acquisition

You need data to train your AI — in this case, facial expressions.

If you use Teachable Machine:

- Click "Image Project"
- Label 3 categories: Happy, Sad, Neutral
- Capture 20+ webcam images per emotion

If you use Python + OpenCV (advanced):

- Use open datasets (like FER-2013 or CK+)
- Or record your own using your webcam

Step 3: Model Building

Using Teachable Machine (no code):

1. Train the model with your emotion data
2. Click "Export Model"
3. Use it in a web app, or embed in a site

Using Python (with code):

```
python
CopyEdit
from keras.models import Sequential
from keras.layers import Dense
# Add your model layers here
# Train using data from images
```

You can use TensorFlow, Keras, or PyTorch if you've already practiced Python.

Step 4: Evaluation

After training, test your model:

- Show different expressions
- Does it predict correctly?
- What is the accuracy (e.g., 85%)?

If the model makes mistakes:

- Add more images
- Ensure balanced data for each emotion
- Check lighting and background

Alternate Beginner Project: AI Quiz Bot (Python)

You can also start with a simple text-based AI chatbot that:

- Asks the user questions
- Learns from answers
- Gives feedback

python

CopyEdit

```
name = input("What's your name? ")
answer = input("How are you feeling today? ")
if "sad" in answer:
    print("I hope things get better soon, " + name)
elif "happy" in answer:
    print("That's awesome, " + name + "!")

else:
    print("Thanks for sharing, " + name)
```

Other AI Project Ideas

Idea	Domain
AI Pet Classifier	Computer Vision
Smart Plant Watering Reminder	Data + IoT
Chatbot for Exam Tips	NLP
Traffic Jam Predictor	Data Analytics
Career Recommender Quiz	ML + Logic

Try It Yourself: Build + Share

Activity: AI Project Portfolio
Create a one-page summary of your project:

- Title
- Problem it solves
- Tools used (Python, TM, etc.)
- Screenshots or code
- What you learned

Share your portfolio with your teacher, classmates, or online tech clubs like ATL, GitHub, or Kaggle Juniors!

Think & Reflect

1. What was the biggest challenge you faced while building the project?
2. How would you improve your AI in the next version?
3. Can your AI help someone in your community?

Let's Revise: AI Project Checklist

css

CopyEdit

Define the problem

Collect and label data

Choose a platform (Python / TM / App Builder)

Train your model

Test and improve

Present your solution

Check Yourself: Quick Review

MCQs

1. What's the first step in an AI project?

a) Coding

b) Data collection

c) Problem scoping ✓

d) Model testing

2. Which platform lets you build AI models without code?

a) Visual Studio

b) Scratch

c) Teachable Machine ✓

d) Excel

3. What improves model accuracy?

a) Less data

b) Biased data

c) More balanced data ✓

d) Random inputs

Short Questions

- What are the 4 steps of the AI project cycle?
- How can you make your AI fair and inclusive?
- Why is testing important before using an AI model?

Explore a Future in AI: From Projects to Products

By building your first AI project, you've already done what many professionals do. Keep going:

Role	Real-World Path
Student Innovator	ATL, CBSE, Science Fairs
AI Developer	Hackathons, online platforms
AI for Good Ambassador	Social projects using tech
Young Techpreneur	Startup idea with AI + impact

Your small idea today can become tomorrow's smart solution for India — or the world.

Abeer's AI Builder Insight
Building even a small working model teaches more than reading multiple chapters. Projects reveal gaps in understanding — and that's where real learning happens.

Beyond the Book: National AI Project Challenge

Project Prompt: "AI for India's Future"

Submit your idea or working project to:

- CBSE AI Project Challenge
- Atal Innovation Mission (AIM)
- MyGov Innovation Hackathons

Focus on a real issue: education, health, farming, finance, or safety.
Make it:

- Useful
- Ethical
- Creative

You are the AI creator of tomorrow.

Bonus Chapter: AI for Social Good – Be the Change with Smart Tech

Let's Begin: Tech with a Heart

Imagine building an app that helps reduce food waste in your community. Or a chatbot that answers questions for elderly people in their native language. Or a model that predicts clean water shortages. AI isn't just about machines — it's about making the world better. In this bonus chapter, you'll learn how to build or design an AI for Social Good project, and how even students can solve local problems using smart, ethical technology.

Explore the Concept: What is AI for Social Good?

AI for Social Good means using artificial intelligence to:

- Help people
- Solve community problems
- Support environmental protection
- Promote inclusion and equality

Goal: Use smart algorithms + big hearts to create real impact.

Identify Local Challenges

Ask yourself:

- What problems exist in your town, school, or family?
- Can AI provide a smart, simple solution?

Issue	AI Solution Idea
Garbage overflow	Image classifier to detect full bins
Lost school days	Attendance checker using face detection
Language barriers	AI translator chatbot

Exam stress	Emotion detector + tips generator
Water wastage	IoT sensor + ML for usage alerts

Focus on simple, scalable, and socially useful problems.

Plan Your AI for Good Project

Step 1: Define the Problem

- What is the challenge?
- Who is affected?
- How often does it happen?
- Why does it matter?

Example: "Elderly people in my neighborhood can't use smartphones because they don't speak English."

Step 2: Design a Solution Using AI

Ask:

- Can a chatbot help?
- Can a vision model recognize images?
- Can data be collected and visualized?
- Is there a simple way to predict a pattern?

Choose your platform:

- **No-code:** Teachable Machine, Scratch + ML extensions
- **Low-code:** MIT App Inventor, Google Sheets + AppSheet
- **Code:** Python + ML libraries

Step 3: Collect Data or Simulate It

Data sources could be:

- Google Forms (e.g., to collect survey answers)
- Teachable Machine (to collect webcam images)

• Public datasets (from Kaggle or government portals)

Make sure your data is ethical, safe, and permission-based.

Step 4: Build, Test, Improve

Keep it simple:

• Test with 5–10 users

• Get feedback

• Track accuracy or usefulness

• Improve step-by-step

Tip: A project that works 70% well and solves a real need is better than a 99% accurate model that helps no one.

Try It Yourself: Student Project Sprint

Activity: "AI for My Family"

Create a mini AI project that helps someone in your household:

• A calculator bot for your younger sibling

• A voice command system for your grandparents

• A homework planner that uses reminders

Use:

• Python for scripting

• Google Sheets + formulas

• Scratch with extensions

• Teachable Machine for speech/image recognition

Student Spotlight – Real Examples

Project: AI Mask Detector

By students in Delhi during COVID-19

• Used computer vision to detect if people were wearing masks at school gates

• Sent alerts to staff when rules were broken

Project: Water Waste Monitor

By students in Maharashtra

• Used low-cost sensors and AI to detect excess water usage

• Connected to an app that sends daily usage reports to families

Think & Reflect

1. Can AI solve every social problem?
2. What responsibilities come with building AI for public use?
3. How would you explain your AI-for-good project to a non-technical person?

Let's Revise

sql

CopyEdit

```
AI FOR SOCIAL GOOD
├── Identify a real problem
├── Design simple AI-based solution
├── Collect ethical data
├── Build, test, share
└── Make real impact!
```

Check Yourself

MCQs

1. What does "AI for Social Good" mean?

a) AI for making money

b) AI to help society ✓

c) AI for video games

d) AI for hacking

2. Which of these is a social problem AI can help solve?

a) Climate change ✓

b) Playing louder music

c) Increasing stress

d) None of the above

3. What is most important in a social AI project?

a) 100% accuracy

b) Real impact ✓

c) Speed

d) Money-making

Short Answer Questions

- What are two examples of AI used for public benefit?
- Why is ethical data important in social AI projects?
- Describe an idea where you could use AI to help your school.

Explore a Future in AI for Good

Role	Area
Social AI Innovator	NGOs, GovTech, global non-profits
Climate Tech Coder	Earth conservation, water, energy
AI Accessibility Designer	Inclusion, disability support
Tech Policy Maker	Ethics, safety, digital rights

Your idea + AI = a better tomorrow.

Abeer's AI Builder Insight

Technology is neutral — its impact depends on how we design and apply it. As future AI creators, responsibility is not optional. It is part of the system you build.

Beyond the Book: Youth Challenge

Submit your project idea to:

- CBSE AI Project Challenge
- National Science Fair
- Google AI for Social Good
- ATL Marathon (by NITI Aayog)

Pitch your solution to real experts — and bring your idea to life!

Summary

AI aur Machine Learning ka Maha Gyaan is a comprehensive, student-friendly guide designed to introduce high school learners (ages 14–18) to the fascinating and fast-changing world of Artificial Intelligence (AI) and Machine Learning (ML). Aligned with India's National Education Policy (NEP 2020), the National Curriculum Framework (NCF 2023), and CBSE guidelines, this book empowers young minds to understand, build, and use AI responsibly.

Through clear explanations, real-life Indian examples, coding activities, and thought-provoking reflection points, students are guided step-by-step to become AI-aware citizens and future-ready innovators.

Glossary of Key Terms

Term	Definition
AI (Artificial Intelligence)	The science of making machines think and act like humans.
ML (Machine Learning)	A branch of AI where machines learn from data and improve over time.
Neural Network	A model inspired by the human brain that processes information using layers and nodes.
Python	A beginner-friendly programming language used in AI development.
Supervised Learning	A learning method where the machine learns from labeled examples.
Unsupervised Learning	A method where the machine finds patterns in unlabeled data.
NLP (Natural Language Processing)	A domain of AI that helps machines understand human language.
CNN (Convolutional Neural Network)	A neural network used for image recognition.
Bias in AI	When an AI system unfairly favors or discriminates against certain groups.
Ethical AI	AI systems that are fair, transparent, private, and responsible.